E 1

DISCARD

I'VE DECIDED I WANT
MY SEAT BACK

"We won!"

August 14, 1961

Bill Mauldin

I'VE DECIDED I WANT MY SEAT BACK

HARPER & ROW, PUBLISHERS

New York

Foreword

This book starts where its predecessor, *What's Got Your Back Up?*, ended in the middle of 1961, and the cartoons are once more accompanied by a running commentary in cases where it seemed that the events which inspired the pictures might have dimmed somewhat in memory. Also, with the exception of the frontispiece, the drawings are again presented in the chronological sequence in which they first appeared and are not grouped by subject matter. The first twenty in the book were drawn during my last year as editorial cartoonist on the St. Louis *Post-Dispatch*.

In mid-1962, I went to work for the Chicago *Sun-Times*, not as its editorial page artist but, by prearrangement with the editors, as a sort of "cartoon commentator," appearing on the column page along with assorted verbal pundits, free to say what I pleased and travel where I wanted, so long as I got my stuff in on time. It has always seemed to me that a cartoonist who stays desk-bound and does not get out, like any other reporter—or recorder—of events, and sniff the world about him, is in danger of falling back more and more upon drawing elephants, donkeys, Uncle Sams, and other devices of our craft which haven't changed much since Thomas Nast invented most of them nearly a century ago.

After three years of our working arrangement, the *Sun-Times* seems pleased to continue it, and I am delighted with it. I go to Washington from time to time, staying long enough to study the denizens there, but not long enough to get involved with them. Every few months I go bouncing around the United States with a certain purposeful aimlessness, mailing my cartoons in daily. Sometimes, in an extra-expansive mood, the paper has even let me run in far fields, assigning me to the memorable Kennedy tour of Ireland and Europe in 1963, and, early in 1965, sending me to Southeast Asia and Russia. Although these trips are primarily for educational purposes and background sketching, occasionally I stumble onto a story and send that back along with the cartoons. A sample or two have been included in these pages. Some authors relieve their texts with illustrations. I try to break up my pictures with words.

BILL MAULDIN

I'VE DECIDED I WANT
MY SEAT BACK

"If I were you I wouldn't wait."

July 28, 1961

During President Kennedy's first year in office, the Russians turned on the cold war with bluster in Berlin and resumption of nuclear bomb testing. Kennedy's hopeful domestic program didn't get far.

We took up nuclear testing again, too, and that was the year of the great fallout-shelter debate. Some debated and others dug. The government provided plans for do-it-yourselfers, and speculators got rich selling family-size sections of sawed-off highway drainage pipe. Even pets were provided for in the mass interment program.

October 18, 1961

November 3, 1961

While setting off bombs with one hand, Khrushchev (remember him?) was rewriting history with the other. Stalin became an unlegend, just as Nikita would soon become an unperson.

"Stop asking for Stalingrad stories! There is no Stalingrad!"

2

"We'll follow you anywhere, *mon Géneral. . . ."*

November 29, 1961

The Algerian mess was still not resolved, and General De Gaulle's domestic troubles did not yet allow him to turn the full force of his intellect upon solving the problems of the rest of the world.

"I said let's have lunch together after
the parade."

January 3, 1962

In the Congo, the United Nations, backed by our government, scuttled Tshombe
for the moment, but he had many powerful supporters, including, ironically,
some of our more conservative Southerners.

"I've decided to hell with what the neutralists think."

January 18, 1962

Everybody was acting out of character. While the Dixiecrats were rallying behind an African politician, peace-loving India overran Goa, and anti-imperialistic
Indonesia began clobbering neighbors for fun and profit.

January 24, 1962

President Kennedy, trying to work out a harmonious foreign policy with the State Department, was repeatedly disturbed by brassy trumpetings from the Pentagon. As Commander in Chief, he imposed censorship on public statements by officers, and was accused, accurately, of muzzling them. Nobody ever did say what's wrong with muzzling the military.

"Good lord, I hope they never unmuzzle *you*!"

February 4, 1962

One of our biggest foreign policy problems, of course, was trying to keep our friends convinced that Red China was a huge optical illusion.

The Opium Den

March 9, 1962

Kennedy and Khrushchev were beginning to get along, which disturbed De Gaulle. He implied that America was being bluffed down by a paper tiger, that we would sell out our allies, and that Europe had better look to him for leadership. (Later, when we found ourselves at loggerheads with Russia, De Gaulle accused us of warmongering. He is very hard to please.)

"I tell you Khrushchev is chicken!"

March 13, 1962

Edward M. Kennedy decided to enter public service. He might have been immodest, but three years later it's beginning to look as if he had a lot to be immodest about. He could well turn out to be the best politician in the clan.

"I *am* working through the ranks. I'm starting with the Senate."

"See? Fidel promised to give us what we never had before."

March 14, 1962

After three years of Castro, everybody in Cuba was getting hungry equally.

March 22, 1962

Things were not so equal in South Vietnam, where we were faced with the miserable choice of underwriting tyranny or chaos.

"Personally, I find it a rather unrewarding job."

March 25, 1962

The natives were restless everywhere. A Latin-American politician in an OAS meeting said that his government had become so aware of the Communist menace that it was going to try to collect a few taxes and build a hospital or something.

"Paw, I've come back to get sis."

April 1, 1962

The movement for reapportionment of power in the state legislatures was gaining momentum. Paw couldn't stop all his boys from leaving the farm for the glittering city, but he sure meant to keep the useful member of the family in his kitchen, where she belonged.

April 15, 1962

Another test of strength was between JFK and Big Steel, which decided to raise its prices, then was induced to change its mind.

"What's the nice kitty doing up there?"

May 1, 1962

President Kennedy was mystified by the reaction to his handling of the steel crisis. He tried to pacify the nation's businessmen by assuring them that he didn't think they were *all* s.o.b.'s.

May 2, 1962

Businessmen weren't the only ones in an uproar over administration policies. The New Frontier was for Medicare, and the American Medical Association was rallying its troops to the barricades.

"What happened to you?"

May 6, 1962

If Kennedy sometimes appeared bent on getting between people and their profits, historians will note that he kept vigorously after labor, too, in his efforts to hold down the inflation spiral. His lines of communication with labor seemed, at times, more direct.

May 15, 1962

Another election year rolled around, and once again the rednecks were so preoccupied with gimmicks to keep the black folks from voting that they somehow never had time to improve their own minds.

"By th' way, what's that big word?"

June 17, 1962

In another part of the totalitarian world, there was a rash of escape attempts by young East Berliners. Some didn't make it.

"Personally, I don't cut notches for kids under twelve."

"After we get its attention, we'll teach it obedience."

June 24, 1962

It was during this time, in mid-1962, that the Goldwater people really got going in the effort which won the nomination for their man two years later.

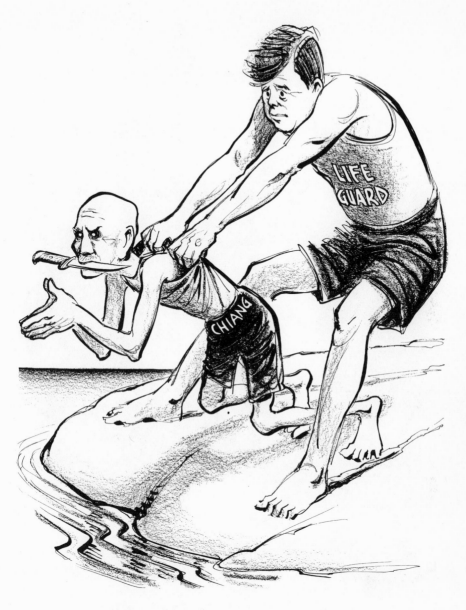

The Old Man and the Sea

June 29, 1962

Late June is bathing season in Formosa, but not for aspiring channel swimmers. Kennedy decided he had enough problems without rescuing Chiang's would-be invasion army from the sharks.

"Man, it's all ours."

July 1, 1962

Africa was exploding with independence and nationalism, and in all too many cases the departing colonial powers had done little or nothing to prepare their subjects for self-government. The "black gang" from the boiler room suddenly found itself on the bridge with a lot of mysterious navigational equipment.

"This is fun, Charles. Are you sure
nobody can see us?"

July 6, 1962

Nationalism and raw ambition were not confined to the leaders of the fresh
young nations. A pair of highly seasoned old practitioners up North were
figuring how to run Europe to suit themselves.

July 15, 1962

Republicans such as Eisenhower, Rockefeller, and Nixon hoped to help the G.O.P. win back some Senate and House seats in 1962 by appealing to the broad center of opinion, but Barry Goldwater, establishing himself as a no-nonsense conservative, was determined to put some zest into what he considered a mess of pink lemonade.

"It's only feathers."

July 21, 1962

August 12, 1962

One of the diversions of the cartooning game is thinking up symbols for people. In portraying the 1962 jockeying for position in the '64 presidential sweepstakes, I found it easy to put Rocky in a Rolls, Barry in a surrey-topped relic and Romney in a Rambler, but what about Nixon? Then I remembered his famous Checkers speech of a decade before.

"Beep! Beep!"

Antimissile Missile

August 16, 1962

Prominent news items in the summer of 1962 were new Russian triumphs in manned space flight (Vostoks III and IV orbited 64 and 48 times, respectively, both landing on August 15) and the fact that our own rocketry was being crippled by strikes and sloppy workmanship. In the midst of all this the head of the AFL-CIO, with his usual tact, came out for the short week as the panacea for technological unemployment.

22

Shadow

August 17, 1962

Perhaps it wasn't altogether accurate to portray the Muslims as a "black Klan" because they don't wear hoods, but in spirit I felt this drawing was fair.

August 19, 1962

The first communications satellite, conceived and developed by private industry, was put into orbit by a government rocket. Senator Wayne Morse of Oregon decided that this made the satellite Federal property. He felt so strongly about Telstar that he actually employed the filibuster, a favorite weapon of the Dixiecrats, Morse's old enemies in the civil rights struggle.

"Baby, I hope you never find your glasses!"

August 25, 1962

One of the problems of dependency is that you have to listen politely when your benefactor offers advice.

"Coming, Comrade!"

Security

September 14, 1962

"See you in church."

September 16, 1962
Things started getting really rough in Dixie . . .

The biggest civil rights story of 1962 was the rioting that began on Sunday, September 30, at the University of Mississippi in Oxford, where James Meredith, a Negro student, was determined to enroll, backed by the United States Government.

I am a weekend pilot when I can afford it, and had flown a small, rented plane from Chicago to Oxford on Saturday, the day before the riot. My com-

"Ain't them fun-lovin'
schoolboys a riot?"

panion was Hoke Norris, the Chicago *Sun-Times* book critic. We were looking for atmosphere, not excitement. Hoke is a Southerner by birth and a William Faulkner fan, and I was merely curious about the place. We knew trouble was brewing, of course, but expected it to come on Monday, the day Meredith was scheduled to arrive for enrollment, and intended to be long gone by then.

We got a Hertz car at the Oxford airstrip, and spent a quiet, enjoyable Saturday afternoon poking around town and campus. Most of the press which had come to cover Meredith had gone to Memphis for the weekend, and many citizens and students were at a big football game in Jackson. We went to church on Sunday morning. It is a lovely old town, with many pleasant people. But

during Sunday afternoon Oxford began to fill with another type: cars full of hard-eyed, red-necked, whiskey-soaked young men were drifting in from all directions. We decided it was time for us to drift out.

The modest landing field, which had contained a handful of light planes the day before, was unrecognizable. It was now a military air base. Our little ship was surrounded by hulking cargo planes, with a dozen more circling to land. As we wondered how to extricate ourselves a Lockheed jet transport from Washington landed, its engines screaming in reverse on the short strip. It discharged Nicholas Katzenbach, the then Deputy Attorney General, and Ed Guthman, Robert Kennedy's press aide.

Guthman, whom we knew, told us that Meredith was coming in a day early, for strategic reasons. The idea was to get him onto the campus before a mob could organize. Shortly after that, the young man arrived in a chartered plane. He looked terribly small and vulnerable, with a brief case in his hand, presumably full of homework. He was driven to the campus, convoyed by several hundred U.S. marshals in Army trucks, and followed by Hoke and me, still in our Hertz car. We realized that a book critic and a cartoonist are not an ideal reporting team in this sort of situation, but we also knew we were all the *Sun-Times* had in Oxford, and we decided we had better deliver.

It was quite a night on the campus. The events are familiar to everyone, so I won't go into them here, except to observe that there are cases where photographs will never replace drawings. Very few pictures were taken of that mob, for the simple reason that they kicked the stuffing out of everybody they caught with a camera. The sketch on the opposite page (which I did *not* make on the spot) was from our vantage point about a hundred feet from the corner of the Lyceum, at the moment when the crowd first started throwing bottles and masonry at the marshals surrounding the building. On the extreme left, under the tree, you will observe one of the local law enforcement officers searching diligently for overtime parking offenders. When the marshals started firing tear gas back, our part of the mob got the first canister, which was fair enough, since they had thrown the first stones.

As the siege of the Lyceum went on, it looked for a while as if the mob would win, and Hoke and I were grateful we had decided to watch from the outside, not the inside, even though we felt like a couple of Alamo sympathizers in the middle of Santa Ana's Mexican army. This decision also enabled us to get back to the hotel and do our work. Hoke filed his first story to Chicago over the telephone.

Next morning, we covered the riots in town, then found it impossible to get a phone line outside. While my friend stayed behind to see the affair through to the end, I managed to wiggle our plane out from under the monsters' wings, flew Hoke's morning story to Memphis, an hour away, and phoned it in from a booth at the airport. Then I took my drawing back to Chicago, airmail, special delivery, at the dizzying pace of two and one-half miles per minute. I believe the only other journalistic organ gaudy enough to have its own plane at the Oxford riots was *Life* magazine. Our editor cheerfully paid our rental charges.

"Let's offer Mississippi some MIGs."

October 2, 1962

"You ain't gaining much altitude
holding me down."

October 10, 1962

Theoretically, President Kennedy had a friendly Congress. He even professed to admire it. But as far as his program was concerned, it seemed for a while a pretty useless Congress.

"Don't underestimate this magnificent animal."

October 13, 1962

Still holding the prisoners from the Bay of Pigs fiasco, Castro kept raising his price for their release...

"A little higher . . ."

"This is nothing. You should see what we do to people who *don't* like us."

October 14, 1962

. . . Meanwhile, a prominent advocate of getting along with the Communists by giving them what they wanted was getting his lumps as the Chinese moved down on India from Tibet. Krishna Menon was India's defense minister, of all things. Somewhat belatedly, he was fired.

Live Ammunition

October 19, 1962

In Southeast Asia we were beginning to take casualties, and our commitment was growing . . .

"Someday, sis, you'll thank me for hanging around."

October 21, 1962

. . . And in our own backyard the Russians were busily planting missiles in Cuban soil. Our reconnaissance showed some of them could reach as far as Washington or Chicago.

"Drop it!"

October 23, 1962

Kennedy, who had been a badly informed and therefore uncertain President during the Bay of Pigs, handled this crisis with cool daring and statesmanship. As one of his aides put it, "We were eyeball to eyeball with the Russians, and they blinked first."

November 4, 1962

Presumably, when the Russian "technicians" packed their missiles and got out of Cuba, they didn't go away without some loot. This cartoon had real poignancy for me. I had been so addicted to Cuban cigars that I had quit smoking when they had become unavailable a year or two earlier.

"We can get aboard if we hurry!"

November 23, 1962

Back on the domestic scene, the '62 elections were over, and Barry Goldwater was convincing some Northern conservatives that their only hope for success in '64 would be to appeal to Southern reactionaries.

November 30, 1962

The Chinese continued to distress their apologists by clobbering India in the Himalayas . . .

"Something darker, please. The light gets more painful every day."

December 2, 1962

. . . and the United Nations, which should have been free to deal with larger matters, was still bogged down in a patch of African jungle.

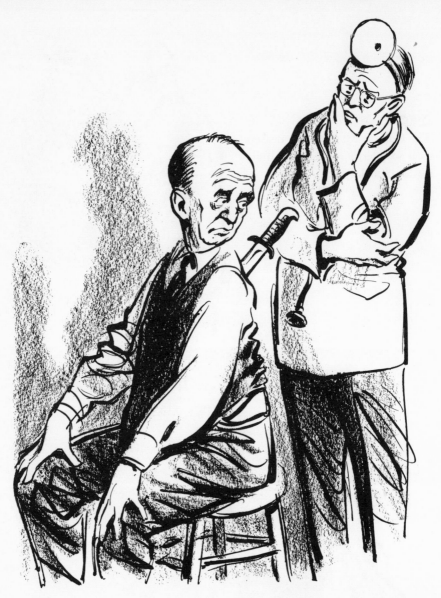

"Judging by the angle, I'd say it came from above."

December 5, 1962

An intimate friend of President Kennedy collaborated on a magazine story which sought to discredit UN Ambassador Adlai Stevenson's role in the Cuban missile crisis. The President was a mite slow in disclaiming the story, thereby slightly tarnishing his otherwise sterling performance in the whole affair. To Stevenson's everlasting credit, he didn't resign.

December 21, 1962

"What are you—some kind of nut or something?"

December 22, 1962

Europeans had nothing against De Gaulle's argument that they were too dependent upon the U.S. for protection. Now, if there were only some way to have their own thermonuclear weapons and have the U.S. foot the bill . . .

"If you need to ask what it costs, you can't afford it."

"Hello, Pentagon? What the hell happened to our air cover?"

December 27, 1962

Twenty months after the Bay of Pigs, and after an extraordinary effort on the part of the Kennedy brothers to raise the "ransom" in terms of medicines, etc. (JFK never ducked responsibility), the prisoners were released.

December 28, 1962

Only a handful of years ago, the enemies of air power were the "battleship admirals." Now, with missiles threatening extinction of strategic bombers, some of Billy Mitchell's boys were behaving just like those stuffy admirals of yore.

"Don't give up the ship!"

January 2, 1963

"It's out."

January 3, 1963

The 1962 census put California ahead of New York in population.

"... And stop calling me 'Shorty'!"

January 5, 1963

"Take your medicine, Chico—it cost Fidel three whole prisoners."

"When I say attack, don't just lean forward."

January 9, 1963

Reports were beginning to leak back that some Vietnamese were more anxious to fight than others. With Madame Nhu behind them and the Vietcong before them, it is no wonder morale was spotty.

January 12, 1963
Normally, I don't use contributed cartoon ideas—I've done it only three times in twenty-five years—but when a California schoolteacher sent in this one about Chinese soldiers in the Himalayas, I couldn't pass it up.

"For all I care, they can give it back to the Indians."

January 17, 1963

Coast Artillery

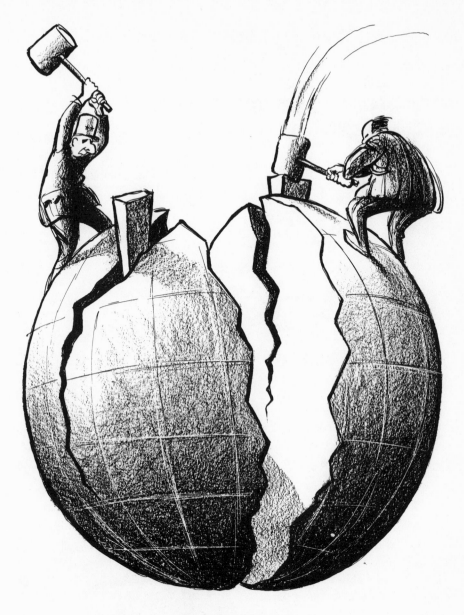

Subdividers

February 3, 1963

March 2, 1963

Another report that began leaking out of Vietnam, and was verified, was that some of our equipment was worn-out, obsolete, and downright dangerous. For a nation whose principal military weapon is technology, this didn't seem very sensible.

Secret Weapon

March 7, 1963

The Reverend Adam Clayton Powell was back in the news with his junkets. A cartoon jibe at this character inevitably draws a hundred or so furious letters from otherwise sensible Negroes. He is not only a preacher; he is a sacred cow.

Congressman at Large

March 17, 1963

Congress passed a bill to make Sir Winston Churchill an honorary American citizen. Author of the bill, ironically, was the late Representative Francis Walter of Pennsylvania, who was coauthor of the McCarran-Walter immigration act and was not noted for his friendliness toward foreigners. Well, he made a good exception.

"Bloody Yank!"

March 21, 1963

Unplanned Parenthood

March 23, 1963
Castro, furious at Khrushchev for backing down in the Cuban missile crisis, began edging toward Mao, ideologically speaking, but never quite forgot where the groceries were coming from.

March 28, 1963

Cartoonists, like everyone, go on kicks. This was my week for hats. First, Defense Secretary McNamara had occasion to reassert his authority over some noisy brass . . .

Top Hat

High Sierra

March 29, 1963

. . . and some modest social reform or other was slapped down in some banana republic. I forget the details, but it made a good hat.

"Relax. It's a rubber rope."

April 6, 1963

Mortimer Caplin, JFK's chief income tax collector, scared the business and entertainment worlds silly by announcing that night club, restaurant, and hotel bill deductions would have to be proven in detail. Ten thousand headwaiters lifted hemlock to their lips—then Caplin relented and said reasonably plausible accounts would do, and it would not be necessary to take a court stenographer and a notary public to every lunch.

"From now on it'll be skimmed."

April 7, 1963

As the tax collector got tougher, a new fact began to dawn: Uncle Sam's purse was not bottomless. The years of largess had taken their toll. A lot of old habits were going to have to change.

April 17, 1963

Freedom of expression took a drubbing on two fronts. Russian artists, musicians, and writers had been given a comparatively free rein during Khrushchev's de-Stalinization period, but now the old man, who shared the views of Truman and Eisenhower on such things as abstract painting, announced that he was going to tighten things up . . .

"You've been acting like a bunch of civilians!"

April 20, 1963
. . . and a few days later, in Philadelphia, U.S.A., the public school libraries were actually, incredibly, pressured into censoring the word "nigger" out of *Huckleberry Finn*. It was a bad week all around.

May 2, 1963

For President Kennedy, dealing with Congress continued to be like nailing custard to the wall . . .

"I *am* pushing!"

May 5, 1963

. . . and for Nelson Rockefeller, who hoped to oppose him in '64, and was taking on a new wife in the meantime, it was slowly becoming apparent that public men don't have private lives.

"I keep hearing bells. First they peal, and then they toll."

May 8, 1963
Dixie was having its dog days. With two words, "Sic 'em," Bull Connor advanced the cause of civil rights by a decade.

"I got no use for a man that don't like dogs."

May 19, 1963
In Yankee territory a question remained. Which is more soul-destroying—to discriminate openly and frankly against a person, as in the South, or subtly, so that he never quite knows what to expect next?

"Up North we sort of nibble 'em to death."

"What do you mean, 'not so fast'?"

May 10, 1963

"Sh-h-h! It's sleeping."

May 18, 1963
Leroy Gordon Cooper made his historic flight and, like any sensible family man, took advantage of the peace and quiet to grab a little sack time en route.

"They're hopelessly divided."

May 24, 1963

I forget exactly why I drew this cartoon, and I hope, historically speaking, that I have to eat it. I think I had just read some pundit who said that, strategically speaking, we could count on a continuing Sino-Russian feud. It seemed to me that, strategically speaking, it is a mistake to count on anybody for anything.

"It's a package deal."

May 25, 1963

A friend of mine who works in the United Nations said that perhaps the best way to appreciate the feelings of some of the new nations which were only recently colonies is to watch a coiled spring which has been held down too hard. It jumps about wildly, vibrates a while, then more or less settles down.

"... And, Sir, can a Protestant put in a good word for the Pope?"

May 28, 1963

Pope John XXIII died, and was mourned by more people of more faiths than any other man, probably, of our time.

June 11, 1963

Harold Macmillan's government was toppled by a scandal so wild and weird that the crummiest magazines would have rejected it as too implausible. It had everything—trollops in the buff in baronial swimming pools, costume parties where only masks were worn, a pimp who practiced medicine, a Russian diplomat, and a prize patsy, Macmillan's Minister of Defence, whose name was Profumo (he had apparently been a gallant soldier).

"King-size or regular?"

June 16, 1963

This cartoon was drawn some time before the Surgeon General's report came out, at a time when advertising agencies with cigarette accounts could still bring a lot of pressure to bear on newspapers. As far as I know, not a single editor who printed the cartoon got any feedback, which indicates that perhaps the cancer peddlers already knew the war was lost.

Bird Sanctuary

June 28, 1963

One of the sorriest sides of the whole civil rights story is that some of the most stubborn holdouts against fair play and human rights are working stiffs. You wouldn't mind so much if it were only landlords and headwaiters.

July 17, 1963

Russia, the U.S., and Britain finally got around to talking about outlawing bomb tests in the atmosphere. By this time, of course, France was sending up mushroom clouds in the Sahara, and China was getting ready to set off a few firecrackers of her own.

July 21, 1963
The administration publicly hit the panic button about the alarming outflow of U.S. wealth . . .

Goalie

July 25, 1963
. . . but some individual capitalists around the country had a bigger problem on their minds—how to keep the sit-ins out and preserve the integrity of their establishments.

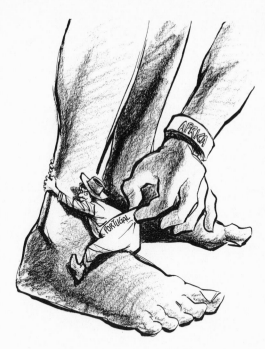

August 2, 1963
Speaking of sit-ins, Portugal had
decided that to be thrown out of
Angola would be a denial of her
own civil rights.

August 11, 1963
Les Americains strike back! At the
instigation of France, the Common
Market slapped a prohibitive tariff
on U.S. chickens. We called their
hand and raised.

Jackpot

August 18, 1963

As sit-ins, kneel-ins, pray-ins, marches, and boycotts continued, their effect became cumulative and it got under people's skins—which was the purpose of the whole thing.

"Man, this stuff's been aging for 100 years."

September 6, 1963

"I've decided I want my seat back."

"Sukarno may be an imperialist, but he's *our* imperialist."

September 21, 1963

September 29, 1963

The Trujillos had never let political talent develop in the Dominican Republic. After they were gone, leadership was scarce and shaky. Juan Bosch, a good but weak man, lasted seven months. (Like Jonah, he got out of this particular fish, and made a curtain call.)

"What could I do? The poor guy was floundering around."

October 2, 1963

Eight days after Bosch's 1963 fall, a junta also took over in Honduras.

"Latin America has always had a high infant mortality rate."

70

October 10, 1963
In Russia, the land of peasants and socialism, they had more money than wheat. In America, the land of bankers and speculators, it was the other way around.

"From each according to his abilities, to each according to his needs . . ."

October 21, 1963
While President Kennedy was selling wheat, the Attorney General was selling something else.

"If we legalize wiretapping, it will end illegal wiretapping."

Never underestimate the power of a woman.

October 27, 1963

Two great ladies wrote two great books: *Silent Spring* and *The American Way of Death,* which upset two great industries.

"It's happened. The machines are reproducing themselves."

November 10, 1963

November 22, 1963

It was one of those days, as with the Sunday of Pearl Harbor, which you remember in detail from then on—where you were sitting and what you were saying to whom when you got the news, what you did then, and so on.

By noon on this particular Friday I had finished my week's work, including a cartoon for the coming Sunday, and had gone with some friends to a luncheon to hear a speech on foreign policy. The speech was never made. Halfway through dessert, the news that President Kennedy had been shot spread through the room. A little later, as we all sat there, we learned that he was dead.

I asked my friends to drop me at the office on the way home. I was amazed at how upset I was. There is nothing like doing familiar chores in familiar surroundings to keep your keel under you. I started working at 2:00 P.M., one hour after the President was declared dead.

What to draw? Grief, sorrow, tears weren't enough for this event. There had to be monumental shock. Monument . . . shock . . . a cartoon idea is nothing more or less than free association. What is more shocking than a statue come alive, showing emotion? Assassination. Civil rights. There was only one statue for this.

I started the drawing at 2:15 and finished at 3:00—the fastest I had ever worked. An average cartoon takes three or four hours. I almost threw it away (after all, my week's work was done, and nobody expected this one) because I couldn't get the hair right. No matter what I did with it, it looked more like Kennedy hair than Lincoln hair. This might confuse some people who weren't familiar with the statue. Then I decided that if they didn't know the statue they wouldn't get the cartoon anyway.

The Chicago *Sun-Times* engravers did a record job, and so did the press room. Our first edition was on the street at 4:45 P.M., November 22, 1963. The cartoon was on the back page, and later I was told that most Chicago news dealers sold the paper with that side up.

75

Lock Step

November 24, 1963
On Sunday horror was compounded by idiocy when the assassin was murdered.

Old Hand

November 27, 1963

December 6, 1963

Advertising agencies, no longer able to sell cancer sticks as adjuncts to physical and mental health, fell back on the fact that a lot of kids start smoking to look grown-up. If you didn't have Brand X hanging on your lip, the girls (or boys) wouldn't look at you, and you might even turn out to be impotent.

"You understand, these things are for us adults only...."

December 13, 1963

They stopped building Studebakers in South Bend, Indiana, and when I drew this picture I thought the old boat had joined the immortals. It went back into production in Canada.

"Not *Studebaker!*"

December 25, 1963

The Berlin wall was opened for Christmas to allow relatives from the West to visit in the East.

January 15, 1964

Our new President flabbergasted the Republicans by proving to be a pinch-penny. He even turned out the lights in the White House. If he kept on this way, they would have to start looking for new issues in future campaigns.

January 31, 1964

In our hearts most of us cheer the new nations of the world on, and remember that we stumbled around quite a bit in our early days, too—but even so, it's hard to resist kidding them.

Student Driver

February 15, 1964

"Is he leaning on it or holding it up?"

February 19, 1964

One new nation decided to go for broke. King Sihanouk, feeling the wave of the future was in the North, renounced American aid and started letting the Vietcong crawl through his woods.

"I'm going where I'll be appreciated."

February 28, 1964

If the Cambodians thought they would hurt our government's feelings by giving our money back, they badly misjudged the new mood in Washington.

(For months, I had been itching to draw a Beatle, and this was as near as I could come to a legitimate excuse.)

"Shouldn't we try the scissors first?"

March 5, 1964

Weapons Inspection

March 11, 1964

"Son, in this outfit you are now *Brand* X!"

March 13, 1964

The Black Muslims split wide open in a power struggle over who was going to be the true prophet, and, presumably, collector of the dues. With Malcolm's assassination the following year, the outfit began to look more like Cosa Nostra than a religious organization.

March 20, 1964

Secretary of Labor Willard Wirtz came up with some depressing statistics to show that in our overcrowded, technological, ferociously competitive society, the day of the successful, self-made, uneducated, Horatio Alger hero is about over. If you want to make it, kid, you'd better stay in school.

March 21, 1964

Unfortunately, all too often the wrong types elect to remain in the classroom.

An Apple for Teacher

"By damn, they'll know they've been in a fight!"

March 22, 1964

"I'm an awakening giant myself. Who'll we have for breakfast?"

April 5, 1964

King of the Mountain

Hail to the Chief

April 9, 1964

Our new President learned a thing or two: don't drive eighty miles per hour, or, if you're going to do it, don't drink beer while you're doing it, or, if you must do both, avoid carrying talkative passengers.

"Get off my back, copper."

April 25, 1964

Castro objected to our continuing surveillance. What right did we have to be so suspicious? Mikoyan had given us his word that those missiles had all gone back to Russia, hadn't he?

"It's good for him—listen to him purr."

April 30, 1964

When Johnson lifted his beagles by the ears, every cartoonist in the United States had a field day.

May 3, 1964

As a sort of carpetbagger in reverse, Alabama's racist governor put himself up for President in the Wisconsin and Indiana primaries. He did well enough to convince many shortsighted Republicans that the "backlash" vote was worth exploiting in the coming national election.

GOV. WALLACE'S YANKEE VOTE

"Man, I'm not ever goin' home."

May 14, 1964

Some Republican professionals probably felt they had nothing to lose, anyway, by playing the backlash game. Running against Johnson was not a heartening prospect.

ELECTION

G.O.P. NOMINATION

Hurdles

Keystone Cops

May 10, 1964

In the spring, when it began to be apparent that Senator Goldwater might run away with the nomination, all the G.O.P. leaders had a chance to show their character. Scranton got indecisive, Nixon finked out, Rockefeller stumbled, and Romney cranked and cranked, but Ike was sitting on the ignition key.

May 29, 1964

De Gaulle started telling us exactly
how to straighten out the mess we
had inherited from France.

"Before you start dealing,
Charlie—where are your
chips?"

June 10, 1964

"If you like it, spread the
word around."

June 12, 1964

By early June in '64, it definitely looked as if Goldwater's early planning and hard work in the hustings would bring him the nomination. Now the regulars began to offer the successful maverick free advice. Understandably, he wasn't having any.

"Eh? What's that? Speak up!"

June 18, 1964

The thing the nation's rural politicos had dreaded most had happened. Henceforth, city voters would have a say in state affairs in proportion to their numbers.

Reapportionment

June 28, 1964

After the United Nations had broken its back in a successful effort to get Tshombe out of the Congo, it began to look as if his government needed him more than he needed it.

"When you said, 'Don't call us—we'll call you,' I really didn't believe you."

July 2, 1964

Inevitably, the civil rights movement began to produce martyrs. After each atrocity, there was strong agitation for what would amount to a new military occupation of the Deep South. It didn't work a century ago, and there's little reason to believe it would work now.

"You want me to stomp some brotherhood into 'em, eh?"

"I always wondered what you guys looked like
underneath."

July 7, 1964

97

Outrigger

July 12, 1964

The G.O.P. convened in San Francisco. If I hadn't been there to watch it, I would have thought that those who described it as a *"putsch"* were exaggerating. They weren't.

July 16, 1964

"Gee, who took my elephant?"

July 17, 1964

"I just happened to be passing by...."

"Hey, Mac, how come we're treading water?"

July 26, 1964

Lyndon Johnson hoped to get nominated and run on a program of peace and prosperity, and this Vietnam situation kept threatening to spoil things.

August 2, 1964

Goldwater knew Johnson was a modest man who only wanted half the road—the middle half.

August 6, 1964

Consummate politician that he was, the President still knew when to get tough, as in the Tonkin Gulf affair. North Vietnam shot at our Navy on the high seas, and we shot back.

"I must have struck a nerve."

"Now, Hubert, don't forget who's got the talkin' end."

August 28, 1964

Johnson tried to make a good show out of the Democratic convention, but there wasn't much suspense, except for a brief moment when he managed to manufacture some doubt about who would be Vice President.

September 6, 1964

Our troubles multiplied in Vietnam. In the North they smelled victory and began pressing us hard . . .

"Call, raise, draw, or fold?"

September 15, 1964

. . . and in the South they had the first attempted coup against Khanh.

"For a minute there I thought we'd lost you."

September 25, 1964

Everybody in Asia was feeling his oats.

"Don't clap yet—maybe the show's just started."

October 1, 1964

China jubilantly blew off her first atom bomb, thereby joining France in the peanut gallery of the Nuclear Club.

New Tooth

Drag Race

October 27, 1964

In the end, Asia faces an enemy far greater than the tired old white man.

October 9, 1964

Our Secretary of Defense came up with the grim news that within a generation, unless something is done to stop the spread of nuclear weapons, the smallest country will be able to make a good-sized bomb for a few thousand dollars.

October 23, 1964

Nikita Khrushchev got thrown out of power, and every cartoonist in the world wept a silent tear. There may never be another subject like him. On Monday mornings, when ideas came hard, you could always think of something to draw about Khrushchev. Farewell, Old Pudgy. If I knew your address, I'd send you a case of vodka, and still be deeply in your debt.

"Harold won, Lyndon's winning, and I didn't even know I was running."

November 4, 1964

The 1964 presidential election was over. At last the people had a chance to vote for a choice, not an echo, and they made their choice.

"Which way to the mainstream?"

Dogies

November 11, 1964

Thanks to Goldwater and the disaster he visited upon his party, Johnson had a mandate, and he meant to use it.

"Why do you Americans stay where you're not wanted?"

November 23, 1964

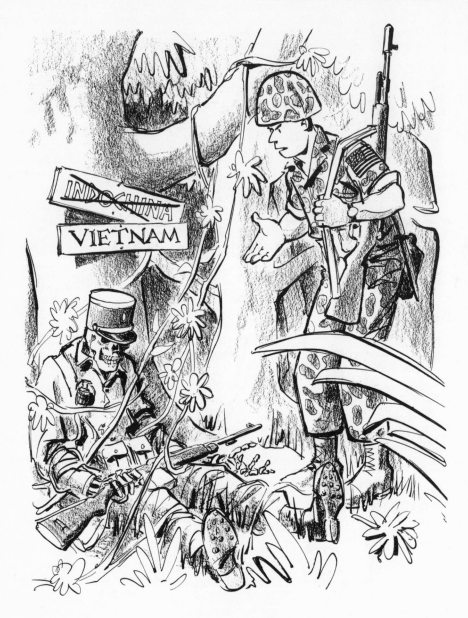

"What's so funny, Monsieur? I'm only trying to
find my way."

November 25, 1964

"We shall overcome!"

November 26, 1964

You can't keep a true believer down. Bumper stickers began appearing with the slogan, "27,000,000 Americans Can't Be Wrong."

December 3, 1964

J. Edgar Hoover made some not-very-well-considered remarks about Martin Luther King, and a perennial question came up: when is Hoover going to retire? A man I know in the FBI called me up after this cartoon came out and said, "Do you mean he has taken root or that his feet are firmly planted on the ground?" I told him to take his choice.

December 9, 1964

It began to be more and more apparent that while the Buddhists might not actually run South Vietnam, nobody else could run it without their approval.

"Will there be anything else?"

December 16, 1964

"Oboy! Just what I
needed!"

December 18, 1964

"Come in, gentlemen. . . .
This way through to India
. . . *Keep moving, please!*"

Heritage

December 20, 1964

December 27, 1964

To the American Medical Association, faced for the first time with a serious threat of Medicare legislation, the issue remained simple: public necessity must wait for private convenience.

"There's a Ford in your future."

January 3, 1965

For Charlie Halleck, the House minority leader and straight man for Senator Dirksen on the "Ev and Charlie Show," the issue was also simple: Congressman Gerald Ford of Michigan had done him out of his job and his chauffeured limousine.

"Who's winning—the forces of freedom or the
people's democracies?"

January 14, 1965

The troops under attack were aviation maintenance men, but they reacted like veteran infantrymen.

January 14, 1965

In line with my theory that people who comment on the tides in man's affairs should get their own feet wet occasionally, early in 1965 I talked the Chicago *Sun-Times* into buying me a ticket to Vietnam. Aside from my curiosity about the place itself, I was anxious to visit my eldest son, who was serving in the Army there. (He was born while I was in Sicily, in another war, in another time.)

I stopped in Hong Kong, bought a new camera I had wanted for years, proceeded to Saigon, and hitched a helicopter ride some two hundred miles north to Pleiku, where my kid was based. I arrived on Friday, February 5, we had a reunion party on Saturday, and early Sunday morning, February 7, the Vietcong gave me its own special welcome. Following is the story I cabled back to the *Sun-Times* a few hours later. The sketches accompanying the text were pencilled during the events and finished in ink later the next day.

The mortar barrage on Camp Holloway and the 52d Aviation Battalion began at exactly 2 A.M. Sunday. It was intense and murderous, some 80 rounds in five minutes saturating a bivouac area, perhaps two blocks square.

The enemy was using captured 81 mm. weapons of our own manufacture.

118

I was sleeping in the east half of a hut house, or "hooch," of Lt. Col. John C. Hughes of Herrin, Ill., the battalion commander, on a cot belonging to Maj. Glenn Parmeter, who is on leave in Hong Kong.

My son, Bruce, a warrant officer and helicopter pilot in the battalion, whom I had come to visit, is billeted in the town of Pleiku, near 2d Corps headquarters which was also hit.

I had just spent the evening in Pleiku having a reunion celebration with Bruce and had left him at his billet.

My first awakening thought at the roar of the mortar barrage was that Chinese New Year was still being celebrated. When a round hit nearby, I realized what was going on and began to worry about Bruce, assuming (correctly) that he would try to get back to his outfit and worrying that the attack might be general in scope, in which case the road to camp would be a bad place for him.

Any further speculation on my part was cut off by Col. Hughes, who roared at me to get myself into the bunker out back, as he tore out the front door to take charge of his battalion.

So emphatic was his order and so positive was my response that I found myself arriving at the bunker barefoot and in my underwear.

The barrage was at its height as I started down the earthen steps to the sandbagged shelter. By the light of the drumming explosions I could see the barbed wire of the southern edge of camp a few feet away, and I fully expected to see hostile faces on the other side moving up under cover of the mortars.

It turned out that the only infantry penetration was to the east, where the parked aircraft were attacked.

A young soldier from headquarters company came up to me at the bunker entrance. He was also in his underwear, but mine

American-made mortars are effective, even when used by the wrong people.

was white and his was red. He was holding both hands over a large wound in his right side and was covered with blood from several lesser cuts. Mortar shells are designed to cut people up and apparently we make good ones.

"Help me," he said, "I've got to lie down."

I tried to help him into the bunker but he refused to come down those dark steps. He said he had decided he was going to die and he wanted to lie down on something comfortable.

From the looks of the wound, I felt in no position to question his prognosis, so I helped him into the hut and put him on my cot, where I found a small light and took a closer look at his side. I couldn't tell whether the large fragment had gone into his guts or had simply cut him open in passing, but hoped for the latter.

At this time, the mortar barrage had been going on for about four minutes, interspersed with grenades and some recoilless-rifle fire. Again I asked my friend to let me take him into the bunker but he was adamant about staying above ground.

"I'm pretty sure I'm going to die in a minute," he said in a real tone of apology, "and I would appreciate it if you would let me hold onto your hand and say my prayers."

What can you do? I let him hold my hand and he recited the Lord's Prayer.

As he finished, the mortars let up and Col. Hughes came in, mad as a hornet. He had seen our light and wanted to know what the blank I was doing upstairs.

"Oh," he said, looking at the cot, "I'll send some litter bearers back."

He went back to his command post. Shortly, four soldiers with carbines came in on the colonel's orders, to help me move the wounded man. Lacking a stretcher, we carried him on my mattress for the two-block walk to the dispensary.

For some reason, I had

Little streams of blood merged into big ones.

Several choppers were destroyed by charges planted inside.

At first light crews of the surviving choppers organized a Vietcong hunt.

stupidly assumed that our boy, who had made his peace with his Maker and was now uncomplainingly enduring the rather bumpy ride we were giving him, was the only casualty in the area.

Now, as we made our way among the riddled "hooches," we found ourselves part of a regular gory procession with hurt men stumbling out of practically every tent, each leaving his special trail of splatters, so that next morning there were scores of little red trails converging into one big one leading to the medical hut.

Most of the wounded were being supported or carried. Few had only one cut and some had dozens. Of the initial five dozen casualties treated, only 18 were walking wounded.

Sometimes it doesn't hurt till later.

Although the mortars had stopped, the war was still on, with a fire fight at the airstrip, where the Vietcong were going after the parked helicopters and twin-engine Caribou troop carriers. There was the thump of TNT, as some of the attackers managed to get charges under the machines.

The dispensary was at the edge of the strip, and when we got there, we could see several aircraft burning.

At no time did I see any sign of panic, even though there was every excuse for panic. An enclosed garrison in a hostile environment had been hit suddenly and hard, and there was no way of knowing if we were going to be overrun. But our new Army seems to be a bunch of pros.

Those who weren't hit had their weapons in hand and were going quickly but calmly about their business, and it is worth noting that later in the morning a number of these were surprised to find blood had run down into their own shoes from punctures they didn't know they had. The first casualty count was seven dead in the battalion and 43 wounded. A later count showed eight killed and 108 wounded.

Inside the dispensary looked like a Technicolor scene out of "Gone with the

Col. Hughes looks over the damage.

Wind." Badly wounded men were sprawled over every bit of floor and huddled on every piece of furniture. Blood was pooled and splattered everywhere and I kept slipping in it as I made my way through barefooted.

Our boy had to give up his mattress because there wasn't room for it. He didn't mind. I believe, at this point, he had begun to believe he was going to make it after all, and this turned out to be right. I told him good-by, he smiled a trifle wanly, and I headed back for the colonel's hut to get my pants.

I believe this was my worst time in the whole affair, because it suddenly occurred to me that in my state of undress I resembled a Montagnard, a local Vietnamese hillbilly, who runs around in shirttails and not much else. This could lead to a misunderstanding in the dark with an armed soldier on the alert for infiltrators. So every time I passed a soldier, I made a point of pretending to stumble, then uttering a four-letter word in unmistakable English.

Back at the hut, I got dressed, found my camera and sketchbook, and went out to cover the war like a gentleman correspondent. At 2:35 A.M., the firing had stopped. At 2:45 A.M., I heard a loud commotion at the front gate, angry voices, and a shot. I never did learn what the shot was about, but the ruckus was created by my son, Bruce, who had come to save his beloved helicopters and was having trouble getting past the sentries.

Later, I watched him help direct operations as the wounded were evacuated by air and told him he was doing a fair job for a man who couldn't even get to his own war on time. He told me to go to hell.

123

February 10, 1965

This cartoon was drawn shortly after the Pleiku attack, when I learned that the enemy mortars had been set up in a friendly village fifteen hundred yards away. The American dilemma at that time was that if we took effective steps to defend ourselves, we became belligerents instead of advisers.

"It Leaks."

February 12, 1965

President Johnson solved the dilemma. He bombed hell out of North Vietnam and we became belligerents.

"Don't forget your commitment!"

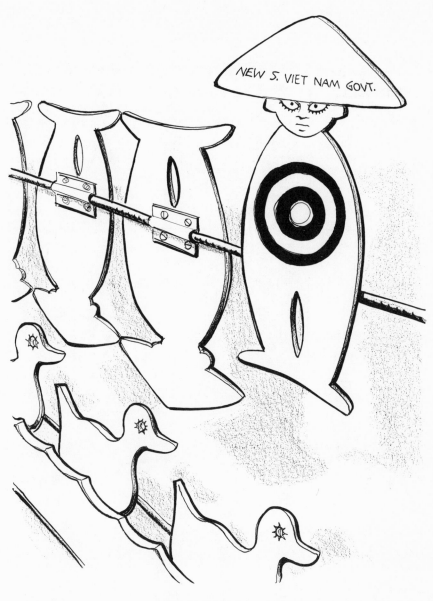

The Gallery

February 20, 1965

Everywhere I went on that trip, I was a jinx, like the little man in the Al Capp comic strip with the cloud over his head. When I returned to Saigon from Pleiku, they had another of their famous coups.

Design for U.S. Embassies

March 2, 1965

I returned home by way of Pakistan, Russia, and Austria, to see how people in these various countries were reacting to our new strategy in Vietnam. Nobody seemed nearly as angry at us as the propagandists said they were, but the jinx was still with me. I had lunch at the U.S. Embassy in Moscow, and next day it was mobbed. (A few days later I landed in Vienna, and within an hour the President of Austria died.)

Second Front

March 10, 1965

I got back to the U.S. just in time for the race troubles in Selma, where the Alabama police made it possible for the President to get a real civil rights bill through Congress.

March 17, 1965

"Little did I dream, when I became President, that I would go back to teaching school. . . ."

March 19, 1965

Project Gemini was a success, even if the Russians did upstage us again.

March 28, 1965

Integration

April 21, 1965

A group of Alabama business leaders, shocked at the events which culminated in the civil rights march from Selma to Montgomery and the murder of Mrs. Viola Gregg Liuzzo, declared themselves in favor of human rights and the twentieth century.

"Let's just say you and I are segregated."

"Whatever it is, it isn't paper."

April 25, 1965
The debate raged on about whether we were doing right in Vietnam . . .

"From the shores of Hispaniola, to the hills of Vietnam . . ."

April 29, 1965

. . . and then the President compounded confusion by intervening in the Dominican Republic. Now critics of our foreign policy had more material than they could handle.

April 30, 1965

Probably never before in the history of American wars have the doves been so aggressive or the hawks so timorous, so unsure of themselves.

"Couldn't we negotiate?"

May 5, 1965

"I admire *all* the Roosevelts."

May 6, 1965

It's hard to figure out an ending for this sort of book in times such as these. Who knows what the Vietcong has in store for us, or we for them, in the suspenseful period after this is written and before it is printed? What new dramatic roles will Lyndon Johnson and Charles De Gaulle decide to play before publication date? Let's have a last, lingering look at our President as the New Dealer at home and the Rough Rider abroad, take comfort in the fact that whatever else might happen to us, we won't die of boredom, and then let's quietly slip the cover over the typewriter.

About the Author

Bill Mauldin's editorial cartoons appear in over 250 newspapers in the United States and Canada. His home base is the Chicago *Sun-Times,* in which his cartoons appear five times a week.

Mr. Mauldin was born in Mountain Park, New Mexico, in 1921, attended public schools in New Mexico and Arizona, and spent a year at the Chicago Academy of Fine Arts. By the time he was eighteen he was in the Army and at twenty-one became famous for his "Willie and Joe" cartoons. By the end of his army service in 1945 he had covered the campaigns in Sicily, Italy, France and Germany, and had been awarded the Purple Heart and the Legion of Merit. He also earned his first Pulitzer Prize.

In the postwar years, Mr. Mauldin published several books and covered the Korean War for *Collier's.*

Mr. Mauldin joined the St. Louis *Post-Dispatch* as its editorial cartoonist in 1958, and one of his first year's crop of cartoons won him another Pulitzer Prize. He joined the *Sun-Times* in June, 1962.

In 1960 the National Cartoonists Society gave him an award for the "Best Editorial Cartoon of the Year"; in 1962 he won their top honor when he was voted "Cartoonist of the Year." In 1964 he won the Sigma Delta Chi award for the best cartoon of the year.

Mr. Mauldin lives in Chicago with his wife, Natalie, and their four sons. An older son by a former marriage is now an army helicopter pilot and has just made him a grandfather.